THE
BOOK
OF
MARVELS

LORNA CROZIER

the BOOK

• • • OF • • •

MARVELS

///////// A /////////

COMPENDIUM

of Everyday

THINGS

GREYSTONE BOOKS

Vancouver / Toronto / Berkeley

Greystone Books Ltd.
www.greystonebooks.com

Cataloguing data available from Library and Archives Canada
ISBN 978-1-926812-75-5 (cloth)
ISBN 978-1-926812-76-2 (ebook)

Editing by Barbara Pulling
Copyediting by Shirarose Wilensky
Jacket and text design by Jessica Sullivan
Printed and bound in Canada by Friesens
Distributed in the U.S. by Publishers Group West

We gratefully acknowledge the financial support of the
Canada Council for the Arts, the British Columbia Arts Council,
the Province of British Columbia through the Book
Publishing Tax Credit and the Government of Canada through
the Canada Book Fund for our publishing activities.

Greystone Books is committed to reducing the
consumption of old-growth forests in the books it publishes.
This book is one step towards that goal.

To Patrick
We are at home with one another;
we are each other's home.

"I suggest that every person open an interior trapdoor, that he negotiate a trip into the thickness of things, that he make an invasion of their characteristics, a revolution, a turning-over process comparable to that accomplished by the plough or the spade, when suddenly millions of particles of dead plants, bits of roots and straw, worms and tiny crawling creatures, all hitherto buried in the earth, are exposed to the light of day for the first time."

FRANCIS PONGE

"A dictionary resembles the world more than a novel does, because the world is not a coherent sequence of actions but a constellation of things perceived. It is looked at, unrelated things congregate, and geographic proximity gives them meaning. If events follow one another, they are believed to be a story. But in a dictionary, time doesn't exist. ABC is neither more or less chronological than BCA. To portray your life in order would be absurd: I remember you at random. My brain resurrects you through stochastic details, like picking marbles out of a bag."

EDOUARD LEVÉ

"You can observe a lot just by watching."

YOGI BERRA

CONTENTS

AIR

LONG BEFORE Alexander Graham Bell or *Sputnik*, air communicated across vast distances. Sand from the Sahara travels on the sky's swift currents to end up in Moose Jaw, where it becomes an irritation in the eye. Atoms from exploding stars fall through space and time, blow through the kitchen screen; they move through our lungs and powder our bones. How many centuries do we hold inside us, how much dying light?

Once, air was not a thing, neither thick nor thin. It was weightless and invisible. The portmanteau word *smog*—air that can be seen—came into common use only a hundred years ago. It smells, of course, but some claim it can be felt, too, like scraps of soiled silk slipping across your face. Frogs are the canaries of the thermal shafts: their skin absorbs the air, and they are dying out. Along with them vanish fertility, transformation, abundance and the springtime theurgy of their songs.

Your friend can't bear the air inside a beauty parlour.
She wears her grandfather's WWI gas mask with its long
snout when she gets a perm. If we had to wear such
ghastly devices on days when we're cautioned against
leaving the house, would we become more radical? Chain
ourselves to fences? Change our habits? Play flutes,
clarinets and oboes long into the night to pay obeisance
to the gods of breath so they won't leave us breathless?

Mistral, Sirocco, Williwaw, Boreas, Chinook, Shoa:
just a few of the names for air in motion. *Wind* becomes
mind with a change of just one letter, but it slips away
from rhyme's halter and bit. It is no one's creature.
Ungraspable, wind is like water moving through water,
or like a thought, before it's found the words, unfolding
in the brain's dark chamber. Though there's a science—
anemology—devoted to the wind, no one can cut it open,
probe its left lobe or its right.

In a certain light you can see smoke from the ovens
hanging over Auschwitz and Buchenwald. You can hear
the rattle of a broken wind passing through the grasses of
Wounded Knee, through the aspens of the Cypress Hills.
You can sight wings of 1930s dust darkly hovering over
the wheat fields of Saskatchewan. Air has a long memory.
It insists we don't forget.

APPLE

AN ALPHABET of things often begins with *apple*. It
goes all the way back to Eden, the serpent's seduction,
Eve's gift. You find the last red apple left in the bowl just
as beautiful, as tempting. Though it has a particular flush
and ripeness, a unique blemish near the stem, it bears the
weight, the import of the original fruit. Adam's crunch
through the peel into the flesh still echoes outside the
garden walls and repeats itself with every bite. Eve bit
too, and what they tasted was desire: they saw each other's
nakedness for the first time. Imagine that—the apple
striking the blindness from their eyes, casting a glow
on the eager persuasion of their skin! Hunger entered
the world then; their bodies blossomed, their tongues
touched. That small grenade of lust you polish on your
blouse and drop into the bag that holds the sandwich
you'll eat later is Eve's legacy to all who multiplied across
the earth.

BED

SOLID. IMMOVABLE. It does little more than take up space in the room it gives its name to, but at night the bed could be any kind of boat—a dory from Newfoundland, Cleopatra's pleasure barge, Noah's ark noisy with mating calls and appetite. Most nights, your bed carries only you and a long-haired, bossy cat. When you nod off between the sheets, the bed unmoors, breaks away from the walls and floats into the dark. The cat's breathing is enough to fill the sails of your sleep; you drift with the drifting boat across the water. Sometimes the night is a harbour, the surface calm and star-struck, feathered heads of ducks and gulls tucked into their wings as they float among the constellations, the bed gliding past. Sometimes the bed bucks and rushes toward a waterfall; you shout in your sleep, but you don't go under. Even deep inside your dream, you know the bed won't tip or sink and you hang on.

At the first sign of morning, the cat touches your cheek with his paw, and the bed slips into its familiar berth, the covers tangled, the sheets damp. When you don't move, the cat claws the mattress right beside your head. Though you're awake, just to show him, you don't rise, you keep your eyes closed. The floor, the walls, the chest of drawers, your heap of clothes—one by one, morning light returns them to the room. The bed has settled. The air is dry as flour.

BICYCLE

BOTH AFTERWORD and foreword, the bicycle leaning
against the fence waits for you to write the in-between
on the wide pathways of the afternoon. Like your grand-
mother's treadle Singer, it needs your feet and the muscles
of your legs to stitch your body to the wind. To the bicycle
schooled in Tao, all distances are near, hills are level, your
knees are no different from an antelope's. Thank god it's
discreet; what it's closest to is your buttocks, each side
in its separate shapeliness, the glutei maximi below the
sacrum and the swell of flesh that makes the hard seat
tolerable on the long ride home. Horses lift their heads as
you fly by. My Pegasus, my long-boned mare! The spokes
find their model for delicacy and toughness in the spider's
web and in the strings of a cello that journeys miles on
the wheels of its own music. The bicycle is an anodyne

for the tentative, the too-long out of use. Don't worry. Whether the fear is singing in a public place after years of silence, diving off a dock into the cold as you did as a child, or falling, as an old man, afraid of the heart's steep cliffs, in love, it's like riding a bicycle. You never forget how to do it.

BOBBY PINS

THE MAN who invented them adored his mother and, later, his wife. The proof is in the hours he devoted to preventing the hair pin from scratching the scalp. After many experiments with the family's St. Bernard, he came up with plastic polyps, the size of the head of an ant, to cover the tips. Run your finger over them to see how finely they fulfill their purpose. What ingenuity, what premeditated care! He'd be the first to admit bobby pins are dull and unattractive. Still, he had an eye for beauty. Look at what they do—expose a woman's neck, modestly reveal the delectable whorl of an ear. They're responsible for that intimate command, "Let down your hair." After, at least one of them goes missing. When it's found days later under the bed or inside the pillow slip, it carries love's rusted lustre, that small ache.

BOOK

NO MATTER what's inside it, there are certain things each
has in common with all the others. The back cover and the
front, the quire of pages, the nerveless spine. A book talks
to you as you'd talk to yourself alone. Each one affirms
there is an end to things. The last page is often blank, but
few readers have the courage to fill it in. Eventually, the
book demands of almost everyone a special pair of glasses.
This takes a lot of cheek. Otherwise, though some have
changed a country or a life, books are humble. They travel
in a worker's pocket or in a backpack, nestled in a bundle
of gamy socks and tired underwear. All are lessons in
failure and forgetting, yet they build "the greatest things
from least suggestions." Ignore the genius or longevity of
those who pen them: it is the book that lasts, uncribbed,
uncoffined. There's something heroic and sad about the
nom de plume printed horizontally in several places
and running vertically down the spine. To the book, the
letters of the name, though often gilded, spell Anon.

BOWL

OLDEST AMONG dishes is the bowl, its shape found in shells and rain-eroded stones; in puffballs sliced in half, gills gutted; in hollowed-out homonyms that grow on trees, mainly oak and maple. There are four qualifiers essential to a bowl's condition: empty and full, whole and broken. These also apply to a human life. The bowl is praised for its compatibility, willingly nesting inside another bowl, tidy denizens of the crowded cupboard. Its specialty is soup, but it welcomes anything you give it. If you spit in it, it remains courteous and restrained. It feels relaxed among aristocrats at court, among the homeless in church basements, at the feet of a busker who sings for coins. It shows no preference for humans over cats or dogs. Though it looks satisfied with its fate, one of the usual dishes in the customary setting on the table, the bowl has more in common with the dragonfly than with the cup or pitcher. Few know it is a rarity counted among the special ones capable of shifting shape. Its stage right now is pupae. Under the proper conditions, it will meta-morphose. Become a horse's hoof, an ocarina, a set of porcelain teeth shining in a glass of water by a bed.

BRAIN

1. Over and over, it quotes Descartes, "I think, therefore I am," though it doesn't really know what it is. Like a looking glass, it cannot see itself. It knows its shape and size only from images of other brains it's glimpsed in books and films or on computer screens, though once there was a picture of it backlit on the wall in a doctor's office. These sightings have led it to consider several metaphors: a walnut minus the shell, a cauliflower turning grey and soft, the bioluminescent cap of a Brazilian mushroom, recently discovered, that glows green in the forest at night. Here, the brain halts the thought and corrects itself: in the dark bowl of the skull, it glows blue.

2. The brain believes in ghosts. It knows they exist because it creates them. A missing arm or leg, its phantom pain strong enough to make a grown man bite into a piece of leather. A stolen child, her cries tucked into a grey cerebral pleat. The brain hears the sound every night and sends it to the heart, which—though this is biologically impossible—aches.

3. Lean and hungry, the brain thinks too much. It plans and ponders and rehearses and resents and worries and conspires and worries and regrets and divides and supposes and forgets. Then there's the dreaming. Every night it creates an emporium inside the head, a mental cirque du soleil, a solar system yet unnamed, with all its suns and moons and people from the past: a bus driver met only once, a mother pushing a carriage full of cabbages, a boy thin and beautiful as a cheetah, a lonely child who is merely the sleeper growing old.

4. The brain's right frontal lobe is the seat of the *Homo sapiens'* sense of humour. Those with lesions there often exhibit euphoric behaviour and inappropriate laughter. They love slapstick. Given the choice, they'd rather spend an evening with the Three Stooges than with Mary Walsh or George Carlin. To map humour's brainy home address, scientists have designed a test, a joke with multiple punchlines.

> A teenager is being interviewed for a summer job.
> "You'll get $50 a week to start off," says the boss.
> "Then, after a month, you'll get a raise to $75 a week."
>
> Punchline selection:
> a) "I'd like to take the job. When can I start?"
> b) "That's great. I'll come back in a month."
> c) "Hey boss, your nose is too big for your face!"

You can guess which option right-frontal-damaged
patients are likely to choose. And which one those with
uninjured brains pick. But who would choose a)? Has
their brain damage been undiagnosed? Are their wounds
invisible? Can you imagine how boring they would be as
mates, even friends you'd meet once a month for lunch?
Wouldn't you rather put up with a cushion that farts, a
brother who slaps the sibling behind you when you duck,
a banana peel left every night in the middle of the hallway
that leads from your bedroom to the bathroom door?

5. Meanwhile, the body. The brain forgets it is simply one
   part. It sits high on its throne and commands. Sometimes
   the legs won't move and the brain throws a fit. Makes
   the teeth bite through the tongue, the eyes roll back,
   the limbs thrash like those of a swimmer who's thrown
   himself into an arctic sea. Face it. The brain is a bully, a
   buffoonish brute that loves to alliterate. It is buff from
   hefting all those weighty burdens, bruised, belligerent,
   baffled, barren: that's what it comes to, barren. It's not
   the mind, with all its clout, but the rest of the body that
   creates, without cognition, the anoetic miracle of flesh
   and bones.

6. The brain is its own mole, digging in the dirt of dreams. It is its own sea, drowning in dead fish and salt. Since it has never felt the wind, it takes the sky's word for it. As well: sunlight on the eyelids, the brushstroke of leaves across a shoulder, the spit of rain on the forehead. Its synapses hum like telephone wires thickened with hoar-frost. It takes the heart's word for sorrow, the foot's for lost, the thumb's for what-if. Most days the brain is a beggar seeking the currency of the unimagined, some-thing real and solid its speculations can't make disappear.

7. The tongue is a piece of the left frontal lobe severed at some stage of evolution, fallen into the mouth, blun-dering, reluctant. Of limited mental capacity, it would rather taste and talk than ponder. The brain absolves itself, denies, pretends to be no one's keeper. Disowns the tongue when it leaps from savoury to stupid, for no good reason, when it scats the scatological just to shock. The human tongue believes it is more than just a hunk of meat, though it's no different from a cow's or a pig's. If a stand-up comic's tongue were soaked in vinegar like theirs, the brain surmises, its toughness and the smart talk would be leached away.

8. The brain's oldest part, reptilian, basks on a ledge
   balanced atop the spinal cord. Though it likes to sleep,
   its eyes stay open and do not blink. It's as muscled as
   a lizard's tail; a quick flick and you flee from danger or
   throw a punch. It is here, too, that dreams are hatched,
   if you can call it that. Each dream has a single tooth to
   chew through its egg's leather casing. Afterwards, this
   tooth disappears. Soft-mouthed and squamous, the dream
   then rises to the brain's higher chambers and belly-slides
   into your sleep.

9. The brain thinking about itself is thinking about the
   brain thinking. The brain not thinking about itself is
   thinking about the brain not thinking. Many things
   don't have brains, and they do just fine. Trees, amanita
   mushrooms, geraniums, spermatozoa, million-year-old
   stones. The brain thinking about million-year-old stones
   can't help but wonder what's on their minds.

10. "O full of scorpions is my mind, dear wife!" (Shake-
    speare); out of mind, out of his mind, to be of one mind,
    reminded, "And Archimedes, the famous Mathematician,
    was so intent upon his Problems, that he never minded
    the Soldier who came to kill him" (Swift); frame of mind,
    on my mind, you put me in mind of, your mind's eye,
    "The lads you leave shall mind you / Till Ludlow tower

shall fall" (Housman); mind your manners, mind your tongue, if you don't mind, presence of mind, absent-minded, speak one's mind, "Never mind about your hand-writing; but mind you write" (Disraeli); time out of mind, keep me in mind, mind your step, "I wish either my father or my mother... had minded what they were about when they begot me" (Sterne); mind over matter, in one's right mind, mind your own business, mind the stove, the stairs, the rafter—mind your head! I'll mind, I'll mind; "All the efforts of the human mind cannot exhaust the essence of a single fly" (Aquinas); never mind, dear friends, never mind, "Not at rest or ease of Mind, they sate them down to weep" (Milton).

11. Strange, the things a brain can get used to: trepanning, electric shocks, lobotomies, bruising, lesions, hail storms inside the skull. There's now a scan that can detect a trace of iron in the tissues, a sign that the brain once bled. Following a stroke, one of its lobes, until then an understudy, leaps onto the stage and belts out the libretto because the lead soprano has fallen mute. The brain learns to use a metaphoric walker, a magnifying glass to read the writing on the wall. It drags a dead limb up and down its many stairways, learns to live with familiar pieces of itself turned suddenly remote and cold as ice floes. And like ice floes in the northern seas, they drift.

12. Is it possible for the brain to live in parity with the heart?
    Can it feel? Here is a true story: a British neurosurgeon,
    who was also a poet, had to remove a tumour from a
    young man's brain. As the knife sliced into the cerebral
    cortex, the patient cried out, "Leave my soul alone! Leave
    my soul alone!" A chill entered the operating room. No
    one moved. The surgeon, still bent over the patient's head,
    held the scalpel in mid-air. Around the table, all of them,
    religious or not, stared at the brain naked in its bowl
    of bone. Stunned into silence by that cry, they waited in
    the harsh light, afraid the brain had more terrifying
    things to say.

BUT

YOU MEAN the chary *but,* not the one with the double *t,*
slang for buttocks, which may, indeed, be bountiful. This
but signifies no concrete entity, yet bristles with attitude,
leads to disappointment, errors in grammar ("nobody
came but me") and contrariety. You prefer *and* any day.
Children understand the difference, avoid other conjunc-
tions, too, not needing *because*'s claims of cause and effect,
often false; wallowing instead in *and*'s accumulations, one
action, then another, everything happening at once with
no need for *as* or *while. But* is an adult word. Favoured by
politicians, disagreeable, stingy. It cancels good inten-
tions, leaves the almost-adopted dog in the shelter, terror-
izes patients. Told they've been cured, they still wait for
the doctor's dreaded plosive. Say it and you don't need
the rest of the sentence: "I'd give you a raise, but...," "We
plan on buying you that bike, but...," "I want to help you,
but...," and the one you dread will come no matter what
the years, "I said I'd never leave you, but...."

BUTTON

THE BUTTON'S vocabulary is starkly solipsistic. It uses
its self in its two essential actions. That is, button the
button. And unbutton the button. No waste, no extra
syllable. Adjectives are merely decorative, like *small* or
pearled or *wooden*, though *Tender* in front of *Buttons* is
something else. Only a few adverbs will work, and most
shift what-is-happening to what-will-happen-next, as
in "She brazenly unbuttons her button." *Unbutton* has
been the undoing of many marriages and the beginning
of deceit. Pants or blouse, equally at risk. Who's got the
button? At first glance—such an innocent, so familiar
and unassuming. Shackled by thread, buttons predate
the zipper; they're slightly old-fashioned and difficult to
match. They make you think of white gloves and garters
and cigarette filters red as lipstick. "Button your lip," the
blonde says to him unambiguously as she slips out the
door, the key on the nightstand by the bed.

CEILING

THE LIVING ROOM ceiling thinks it is a cloud (well, why
not?), levelled out, on Prozac maybe, or just satisfied with
where it's ended up. Hardly anyone in the house notices
it's there; humans get bored with what stands still, even if
it's hanging above their heads, its weight suspended. To
attract attention, the ceiling tries to be something else:
butter icing that floated up from a rectangular cake, a
risen floor minus the footprints and furniture, a tablecloth
smoothed by a woman's hand. It's happier, though, if it's a
cloud the four walls hold in place. In its neurons it tries to
stir up some weather. What would happen if it released a
raindrop to land upon a page of the book you're reading?
And then another to prove that you're not dreaming.
You'd look up then, wouldn't you? What would happen to
your equanimity if several snowflakes settled on your hair
and lashes? And then the whole ceiling, bit by bit, softly
drifted down.

CHAIR

A WOODEN chair has few choices. It has four legs, a back, arms or not, put to the same good use in rooms shabby or refined. Never mind what goes on around it, what joy or lamentation. It stays serene. Even if someone throws it through a window, it settles on the shattered glass, still cordial, motionless as a bicycle without wheels. It never gets tired of sitting. Zazen going on for months, for years. Like a faithful novice, you wonder if you should ask a question. You are no Neruda with three hundred queries up your sleeve. Besides, what language would you use? The Druidic tongue long gone, Russian seems the best for talking to chairs. All you know, though, are words like *glasnost, vodka, samovar.* The chair seems immutable, but when the seasons shift, you sense a restlessness you recognize, a silent craving. Something inside it wants to break into blossom, or, if it's winter, to welcome along its rungs and edges a shin's width of snow.

When the astronauts first landed on the moon, they found a chair, legs sunk halfway in grit, no footprints leading toward it or back. The wooden seat held the patina of much use. They told no one. Someone had been sitting a long time, staring at the earth.

CHIN

SUCH A funny thing, really. It looks like the plucked bum of a chicken where the tail feathers used to be. It figures prominently, however, in pleas for valour. "Chin up" and all that, and if you change the phrase's stress, you get an exercise practised obsessively in prison yards and boot camps. In fairytales the chin can be a sign of cockiness: "Not by the hair of my chinny chin chin," proclaimed the first two little pigs. They were wrong and were promptly eaten. If they'd been chinless wonders and fled the scene, would they have lived? A cleft in a chin endows a man with special sex appeal. Picture Kirk Douglas. It's obvious, too, that he did a lot of chin-ups before he bared his chest for the role of Spartacus. With regret, you set aside the chin's aphrodisiac allure and struggle to list its other uses. To hang a beard, to offer a whisker rub, to catch a slip of drool, to sprout a pimple prior to that first hot date? One thing's for certain. On every face, vulnerable or stoic, radiant or sad, the chin serves to hide, with its plump cushion, the grim memento mori of the naked lower jaw.

CLOTHES HANGER

NOW A REPLICA made from a single wire bent and
twisted, once it was a glyph in the secret alphabet of the
domestics, those who scrubbed and starched and picked
up, picked up after. It was the sign they used in friezes
and in margins of sacred manuscripts to ask a question,
usually why. Hence, though the shoulders of hangers are
hidden, one after another they slide along dowels on a
cryptic punctuation mark: ?????????????, always visible.
No linguist or engineer has found a shape that will serve
as pragmatic and philosophic a purpose: that is, hang
up clothes and, at the same time, bring to your attention
in the narrowness of closets the multitude of questions
whose answers you don't know.

COFFEE POT

PERFECT WEAPON in a fight. Once, during a literary festival in Vancouver, a famous Scottish poet cracked a coffee pot on her husband's head. Thank goodness the coffee wasn't hot. Nevertheless, he flew home to Glasgow the next day, four stitches spidering widow's peak to eyebrow. The coffee pot hadn't caused the argument. It was simply close at hand. Most would agree, however, on its appropriateness. No other object in the kitchen can evoke such outrage. Who left that last burned inch in the bottom and didn't bother making another pot? You'd rather scoop out the litter box with bare hands than empty the filter one more time and rinse it clean. This makes no sense, but that's the way of it. The person who poured the last cup and walked away destroyed a marriage, brought down a convent, drove the ancients from their household shrines, leaving the kitchen godless and unblessed.

STARTS WITH
THE LETTER K

IN THE LAST novel by the famous author, the main character, Barney, who might be an alter ego, stumbles around the kitchen, trying to remember a name. A receptacle used in cooking, not every day, often stored in the back of a cupboard, the size of your average saucepan. Something like kohlrabi, Kalahari, kemo sabe, Kalamazoo. Never beautiful, made of plastic or stainless steel, sounds like philander and Ann Landers. Finally, yes! he gets it— *colander*—the word flames like a struck match in the musty cubbyhole of his brain. But what's its use? He picks the thing up by the handle, turns it over and then upright. He puts it on his head. A bicycle helmet, hole-pocked by hail? He takes it off, sets it on the counter. A container to hold a plant that needs drainage? What's its use? What's its use? Panic ricochets like a small hard ball inside his cranium. Doesn't it have something to do with Marco Polo, or maybe the Greeks? Ah, that's it! He laughs in the darkness of the kitchen and stares at the colander—it's a soup bowl, of course, he says out loud, an Ovidian soup bowl (how proud he is to remember Ovid) turned, because of some deity's angry mischief, into a practical joke.

COLLAR

COLLARING THE CAT: try knotting water, braiding
the wind, threading snowflakes among the crystals of
a chandelier. The collar must be made from mercury
or moonlight, strung with tiny bells the cat teaches not
to ring.

CROWBAR

YOU HESITATE to refute Shakespeare, who called it
"iron crow," but you see it as a petrified snake, neck arched,
forked tongue strong enough to pull nails from wood and
spit them out. Hanging on the wall of the shed, it could
be a cane, rusted and heavy, designed for you to take on
a walk through a nasty neighbourhood, the lights blown
out, the garbage burning. Heft it in your hand, and you
come close to feeling the seduction of a gun. It can smash
the hoods of cars, jam under floorboards and yank them
up, rip drywall from studs, shatter windows, crack any
skull you introduce it to. It's less subtle than a wrench,
cruder than a skill saw, harder to control than a hammer.
Among the most primal of tools, it was forged in fearful
symmetry in Blake's blackened furnace. You try to see
some humour in it, a trick or sleight of hand. Bent on
demolition, bluntly inept at building anything you need—
ambiguity, paradox, even the simplest of narratives—it
allows you just the opening of a joke: two crows walk into
a bar...

DARKNESS, ITS ORIGIN

BEFORE THERE was anything, there was chaos, and chaos was not darkness but light. Darkness came next because light needed a companion. It needed, as well, to know what it was by seeing something other than itself for a good part of the day. Light removed a bone from its own rib cage so that darkness could appear, narrow and long with the consistency of air, no marrow in it. Soon darkness expanded, became its own being, found places to hunker in when light walked the world. Then came its creatures: upside-down things, animals with masks, others with naked tails and little claws, big-eyed birds that flew without a sound, flowers that bloomed only for the blind, night crawlers. The darkness inside people grew, too. It settled and deepened in the small simulacrum of the place where it was born, that gap in the ribs closest to the heart, and the heart, neediest, most susceptible of organs, developed the muscle to draw it in.

DICTIONARY

SHE ADORES the dictionary so much, she wraps her
legs around it. She tries to give birth to it. "My son, the
dictionary," she wants to say. This is why she's childless.
She expects too much. A dictionary! What baby would
fall into the midwife's hands spewing all those words?
Let alone the phonetics, the derivations, the parts of
speech. Is it the entries' unbudgeable order she's smitten
with? *Tuba* will never appear before *sassafras, muck* before
lugworm, and every one of them, from the double-volumed
Oxford that suicidal lexicographers rope around their
waists before they walk into the ocean to the concise a
new immigrant carries in her purse, begins, as you'd
expect, with *A.* This predictability could be a bore, but
what makes up for it, she insists, is the volume's gener-
osity, its cold-blooded genius. *A*'s opening definition, "The
first letter of the alphabet," is followed by a minimum
(depending on the edition) of five entries, including "the
sixth note of the diatonic scale of C major"—you *need* a

dictionary, unless you're Gould, to know that. (You write down "diatonic" to look up later.) What comes next are AA and AAA and some famous people's names, building up suspense for the arrival of the first common noun, which—cue the drums—is *aardvark*. Yes! It's an animal—that's not news to you—but what kind? "A nocturnal, insectivorous, badger-sized mammal having large ears, a long snout, and a long tongue, native to sub-Saharan Africa." And now, along with *aardvark,* you've got *insectivorous* to mate with your mouth and tongue. Dictionaries make you younger, she'll tell you. You become a kid again who's falling for the names of dinosaurs. But the best is yet to come. If the beginning knocks you out, wait till you reach the end. In the *Canadian Oxford Dictionary,* second edition, the final entry, she says, is *zzz,* the sound of snoring. How great is that? How much more human, how much more Shakespearean ("our little life is rounded" and all that) can it get?

DOORKNOB

1. Two things that need each other: the mouth and the ear,
   the left foot and the right, the wind and the listing hawk,
   the doorknob and the hand. Yet doorknobs dread the
   human touch. They have a phobia about germs, especially
   the knobs made of glass common in the 1940s, after the
   war, a sign of class in small stuccoed houses with big
   radios and ottomans of fake leather. To respect their fears,
   you'd have to wear a glove or, with a chamois, rub away
   the invisible bacilli you leave behind. Who has time for
   that? Anyway, you'd be pushed aside by people in a rush.
   You'd be mocked and laughed at. Best not to dwell on
   it. There are whales, after all, and disappearing salmon.
   Disappearing doorknobs? That's a laugh. Like rats,
   they've adapted. In fact, their population's gone berserk.
   Count the new skyscrapers, the condo developments
   eating up the fields and marshes at the edges of cities.
   Tally up the multitude of doors. Measure, if you can, the
   dread each building holds.

2. All doorknobs are twins, joined at the centre by a bolt narrow as a pencil, inflexible, unvertebraed. Though they move as one, they never get to see each other. They are like siblings separated at birth by war, by a wall of stone and razor wire. Neither speaks of this. One turns; the other turns. One is outside the room; the other, in. If the door is the entrance to a house, one shimmers with rain; the other is dull and dry. One is often cold or hot; the other basks in the temperate climate of the thermostat. Does anything pass between them? Does a rumour, a memory, a snatch of song run through the metal spine like an electric shock when the door is opened? Perhaps they desire different things and loathe each other. Each knob wanting, above all else, not to turn in the same direction as its double on the opposite side of the door.

EGGS

YOUR FRIEND, who suffers from despair, sometimes composes a gratitude list that starts with the first letter of the alphabet. Her intention is to make it to the twenty-sixth, but she always stops at *e*. So far, that's sufficient. "*E* for eggs" gives her enough good feeling to turn on the light and find some shoes.

ERASER

THE ERASER on the tip of the pencil saves the writer from ridicule and shame. There's no reward for that; rather, while the writer's ego grows with her brevity, her bon mot, the eraser shrinks and hardens. An overdose of lead causes it to sicken. It becomes uncertain and begins to smudge a line, its pink fading to a dirty beige. The pencil, without fail, survives the eraser. The writer gets more confident. "Lay, lady, lay" is not corrected. "She said breathlessly" stubbornly remains. Not to mention lapses in judgement: too many "dears" in salutations, an infestation of *x*'s and *o*'s crawling across the bottom of the page. Without the eraser, without that little porcine snout that truffles out excess and cliché, without that rubbery nippley nub that mercilessly muzzles metaphor, mixed or not, it's like really, really bad. Totally.

FEET

O FEET! Nethermost telluric twins, they are closest to the earth in all their doings. We go where they take us. Naked, they walked us from the sea, our spines straightening, our gills slamming shut, the salt on our skin crusting in the dry air, our hands astonished into being hands and not another pair of feet. Simplest of mechanisms, yet they contain enough bones to construct the skeleton of a small lizard, with some left over in the make-a-reptile kit.

When exposed, feet are more vulnerable than any other private part, more tender. If you fall for your beloved's feet you'll never leave, though the arches will collapse, the bunions bulge and callus. The feet say more about the ungainly state of the heart than the mouth does, than the hands. To suck a big toe is the first and last infinitive in the body's sutra of pleasures.

Some evolutionists believe our olfactory devices are mislo-
cated: they should be in the feet. Oh, what the soles could
tell us: the comings and goings across the grasses, the
sidewalks, the forest floor, the numbing water in the creek.
What does a waft of rain-washed pebbles say to the heel?
What scent in the mud startles the baby toe?

There are days when the feet demand wheels or blades.
They scare you with their daring as they fly across the ice
or whirl along wood and concrete. There are days they
want six-inch stilettos and a marble floor. Older than the
oldest dog, they can learn new tricks. The tango, the tap,
the rubber-boot dance of the diamond miners. But beware
of their confidence, their persuasions. Don't believe they
can walk on water. Convince them you are content with
the modest daily miracle of walking on the earth.

FLASHLIGHT

IT FEELS neglected. Too often it's merely a case for carrying dead batteries. And you swear at it, bang it against your palm. Violently push the switch back and forth as if your anger could charge it up. In truth, it's had enough. It wants to give up its nighttime walks with you, become something more crucial, perhaps a streetlamp in a parking lot, a lighthouse. Even in miniature, standing on end at the edge of the pond, it could save a sailor. Don't fight it. Unlike you, it knows what darkness wants. How at night in the garden a small, brief beam could guide the lost, the invisible—the luna moth, the soul on its new wet wings, the nearsighted mole whose nose ends in an unlit star—safely home.

FORK

1. Beware of people born with silver forks in their mouths. They're rich, and furthermore they never speak the truth.

2. Which came first—the fork for lifting hay or the one for raising food to the mouth? The present-day fork on the table has lost its agrarian connections. It doesn't know *bucolic* from *buffoon* or *bubonic plague.* Can't distinguish popcorn chicken from free-range. It has no affinity for alfalfa.

3. Predictably, in any argument, the fork sides with the Left. At every setting, it's the loner. It can't avoid its companions in the dishwasher or the drawer, yet it feels more kinship with the ornery, the delinquent. "Fork it over," it commands, outlaw to the spoon.

4. The knife undoubtedly divides, but when it comes to
   roads and rivers, it's the fork that makes the difference.
   It's the only kitchen noun, turned adjective, attached to
   lightning. It calls down storms fierce enough to smash
   a mirror inside the house, ignite a broom, blacken the
   silverware, the discolouring dismissed as simple tarnish.
   Just before the thunder when the air turns green, on the
   closed piano by the bust of Beethoven, the tuning fork
   starts to ring.

FRIDGE

REDEEMER IN the kitchen, the fridge saves everything
that can be saved. Its door has weight. Few others, except
a vault's, shut with such solidity. By nature, habit and
intention, it likes its privacy. Perfect in posture, it contains
two countries: one locked in early spring, perpetual and
chilly; the other set in a northern latitude of ice and
hoarfrost. It knows no change in seasons, no dawn or
dusk. Undistracted by the ironic, the unrealized, all day
it toils without emotion. Some believe it is a machine for
manufacturing *now*—the food inside it eludes the future,
almost successfully. In the dark of a kitchen, its door
open, it casts its light on Colville's naked man and woman
who've come from the bedroom to get a glass of milk. At
night, the rest of the house sunk in quiet, the fridge hums
unpleasantly and sometimes trembles. Its dream is the
dream of the dead whose bones can't shake the cold.

GLOSSOGRAPHY OF G

LET THERE BE geraniums, gerbils, gutters, galoshes,
gizmos, gramophones and goo. Let there be Girl Scouts
strumming green guitars in graperies in Grenada. Let
there be gimcrackery among the grackles. Let da Vinci
paint another *La Gioconda*; let gingivitis be cured by
gingerbread; let the Gorgon repopulate the garden with
garter snakes and glass. Let there be god, god, god, all
good and gladsome and Glaswegian, enough of them to
pay attention, a glut of glorious and gosh. Let there be
more Van Goghs, gnus and gnocchi; fewer gnats, germs,
girdles, graves and glee clubs. Let gonorrhea go the way
of the glyptodont; let give-and-give take over take. In
spite of grime and grim and gruel, in spite of gone, gone,
gone, which you and everything you love will be too soon,
with gratitude and gusto let genesis begin with *g*.

GUM

DON'T SWALLOW it, your mother said. It plugs you
up, cleaves to the walls of your bowels for seven years.

In Yli-li, Finland, archaeologists unearthed a five-
thousand-year-old glob of birch-bark tar incised with
the marks of human teeth. Someone who'd listened to
his mother had spat it out. Iroquois chewed spruce and
maple resin; the Inuit, whale blubber; the Mayans and
Aztecs, chicle, the sap of the sapodilla tree. General Santa
Anna, long after his victory at the Alamo, introduced
chicle to his former enemies. Before he gave them gum,
he'd given them all of Texas. You can see why he lived in
exile in New York. The Mexicans wanted him dead.

Toys, bicycle tires, rain boots—that's what the inventor
Thomas Adams tried to make from Santa Anna's gift.
When it failed as a substitute for rubber, Adams built the
world's first chewing gum factory on Staten Island. His
patent was issued on February 14, 1871. The flavour he
added to the sticky gunk churning in the vat was licorice.

He called the new sensation Black Jack gum and though
he's gone, it's still around, charcoaling your spit. In 1906
in Philadelphia, Frank Henry Fleer came up with a varia-
tion that made bubbles. He called it Blibber-Blubber. No
one bought it. Besides its name, its other fault was frailty—
it burst before expanding into a bubble large enough
to matter. Twenty-two years later, one of his employees
improved its sturdiness, dyed it pink, dubbed it Dubble
Bubble and made them rich.

Gum sweetens the breath, wets a dry mouth, relieves
stress, takes the edge off hunger and cleans the teeth, yet
it can egg you on to rude behaviour: slapping saliva-wet
wads onto the underside of restaurant tables; mashing
sticks of Juicy Fruit, mouth wide open, as you chat up a
date or, worse, blowing bubbles between kisses. In spite
of its perils (chomp on gum in Singapore and you'll be
fined) and its ability to incense even the gentlest person,
Americans masticate ten million pounds a year. Cana-
dians chew much less. We also purchase fewer guns. No
one, though *gum* can easily be mistaken for *gun,* has initi-
ated the research that might prove a link.

HANDS

IT'S TEMPTING to start with what they've felt—a dog's ruff, a songbird's feathered throat, the fontanelles on a baby's head, clothespins, mud, the small stones in a chicken's gizzard—but there's too much of it. If touching were a journey, they've been around the world ten times, and they're still travelling. Nothing stops them. They open their own coffins, reassemble their bones from ash. That's why, long after you've forgotten a face, you remember the hands. At night, half asleep, you feel the cold weight of them on your shoulder, your bare back, and in the morning everything they've handled in the room has a glow about it; a shadow, too. The cat looks combed, the locket polished. The ivory mirror your mother left you has been moved to the kitchen table. It lies face down at the place where she used to sit. The ivory is yellowed like your father's fingers where he held his cigarettes.

Your mother, meaning well, said your father's brain was
in his hands. They could fix anything inanimate—not you,
not her, not his own sad life. This morning the window
that was sealed shut for years is open; on the sill, flakes
of paint some tool has chipped away. If you could, you'd
kiss his callused palms, the softness of his inner wrists.
For now, you do what your two hands can do, dig seeds of
sleep from the corners of your eyes, plop two eggs into a
pot of boiling water, pull a chair to the open window, lick
a finger and turn the page.

HAPPINESS

IF HAPPINESS had a body it would be a golden
retriever running through the grass, a shot duck in its
mouth. If it had a taste it would be cardamom, that
bitter seed you bite into at the heart of a jawbreaker, your
teeth and tongue joyfully blackened. If happiness were
a tree it would be the cottonwood ten miles north of the
city where you grew up. Its singularity has given it a
following: coyotes and hawks, grass that thrives in half
an afternoon of shade, couples who need shelter. Immune
from what happens beneath the branches, the cotton-
wood's leaves in the wind make the sound of ecstatic
water, which could be laughter, which could be weeping.

Todd Solondz's film *Happiness* opens with the perfect
family and their perfect grins. The perfect younger
daughter tap dances around the dining room for the
pleasure of the dinner guests. Later, the perfect father
lures a boy into his car. When his perversion becomes
clear to you, it's as if an earwig has been dropped into

your ear and is laying eggs in the folds of your brain.
You remember the insect from a story about adultery
televised on Rod Serling's *Night Gallery* in the early seven-
ties. The cuckold asks his servant to introduce the earwig
and its ways to the lover of his wife. There is a screw-up
in the dark, and the husband becomes the victim. A day
or two later, he can feel the larvae burrowing, eating his
grey cells without end. His screams from the bedroom
drown the orgasmic cries of his wife in the summer house,
and her happiness starts to thin.

Chuang Tzu says fine horses can travel a hundred miles
a day but they cannot catch mice. This makes the mice
very happy.

HAT

1. Not every husband mistakes his wife for a hat. Get that
   out of your head! Look at the hat as a hat—a cloche, a tam,
   a tuque. Married to nothing, an independent item, unlike
   mittens or socks. Some homespun, some outrageous and
   vain with feathers, baubles and puffs; a few even edible,
   like Carmen Miranda's about-to-topple Pisa of fruit.
   When she was trapped in the Empire State Building's
   elevator with ten tourists from Utah, her hat kept them
   well fed until their rescue twelve hours later.

2. On display in the Metropolitan Museum of Art is Elsa
   Schiaparelli's 1938 shoe-hat with its shocking pink high
   heel standing upright, its toe forming a black visor over
   the forehead. Constructed from a sketch by Salvador Dalí,
   it serves as fashion's nod to André Breton and his crew.
   Question: How many surrealists does it take to change a
   light bulb? Answer: A hat.

3. Throughout history, hats have devastated modesty and good taste. They've driven species to near extinction. Mainly birds, who were killed and stuffed to adorn the brims or perch in nests of silk on the crowns. In the Canadian West, because beaver hides made the best felt for chapeaux for European gentlemen, voyageurs canoed the rivers, trading with aboriginal trappers for pelts. These were shipped to milliners in England who hurdled, batted, flanged and carotted, this last step giving rise to the phrase "mad as a hatter." In carotting, workers brushed the pelts with nitrate of mercury to raise the scales on the fur shafts so they'd firmly lock together. The fumes damaged the brain beyond repair. "Oh, yes, mustard! That'll do... Mustard? Don't let's be silly. Now lemon, that's different," said the Mad Hatter.

4. The hat has a mysterious penchant for the letter *b:* bowler, busby, bicorne, Balmoral, bonnet, balaclava, boater, boonie, baseball, beret, bucket, babushka, the Banjo Paterson with its barramundi-skin band. John *B.* Stetson named one of his western classics Boss of the Plains. Magritte's many paintings of the man in the bowler hat further clinch the connection. The centennial exhibition of his work took place in Brussels, Belgium, where the bowler appeared on banners and on buskers' T-shirts on the boulevards. His images have graced the album covers of Jeff Beck and Jackson Browne, but not the Beatles.

5. Not knowing what it was called, many prairie girls wore the fascinator to church in the early sixties. Part of their Sunday best, it was merely a chicken's wing, fully feathered, dyed pink, mint-green or blue, bent and glued to a plastic headband. If you looked closely, you could see the bone where the wing had been broken off. The fascinator was donned the first day warm enough to kick off winter boots and slide your feet into white, low-heeled shoes. Pinched by the plastic band, halfway through the hymns and prayers the bowed, winged heads began to ache.

6. In most houses, hats are relegated to the upper shelf of the bedroom closet. Out of reach, they soon become forgotten. When someone dies, they are often the last of the belongings to go, especially if they're well constructed like the fedora, Stetson or pillbox. There's something about the inside stained with sweat, the hollow space where the head used to be, the particular smell of a beloved's hair that stays in the felt years after.

7. H.G. Wells, on leaving a Cambridge party, accidentally took the wrong hat home and then took a shine to it. The owner had printed his name and address inside along the leather band. Without identifying himself, Wells wrote this note and dropped it in the mail: "I stole your hat. I shall keep your hat. Whenever I look inside it I shall

think of you and your excellent sherry and the town of
Cambridge. I take off your hat to you."

8. To be fitted properly for a hat, the circumference of your
   head must be measured half an inch above your ears and
   the number then divided by pi. That, if you remember, is
   3.14159265; pi is a constant whose value is the ratio of
   any circular circumference to its diameter in Euclidean
   space. Cheaper hats require no math; they come in small,
   medium or large. If you want to wear a tuba on your head,
   as Magritte did in the famous photograph, one size will
   have to do.

9. Some historians believe Napoleon would have triumphed
   at Waterloo if he hadn't worn such a silly hat.

10. Bad hair goes wild for hats. So does baldness. So do
    1920s gangsters and cowboys. The legendary country-and-
    western singer Rex Titter, mobbed by dozens of female
    fans as he made his way from the stage door of the Grand
    Ole Opry to his bus, growled, "You can touch my body,
    but don't touch my hat."

11. The March Hare asked, "Why don't you start at the
    beginning?" It was the Mad Hatter who most reasonably
    replied, "Yes and when you reach the end ... Stop."

HEART

THE HEART can't sever its attachments, no matter how many sutras it hears, how many Tibetan prayer flags chatting with the wind. It adores country folk and their tasks: unearthing potatoes dropped into a tin bucket (how the heart loves that thud), witching a well (how it leaps when the wand dips), leaning into the cow's flank to keep warm, hands pulling the teats with the heart's own rhythm. Like the brain, the heart knows detachment but also ardour. It has more horse-sense and gumption; its memory is lesser and more selective. It's an expert in eschatology: the farewell kiss on a mother's eyelids, the final sigh of an old dog who couldn't get up, sunlight trapped in a house with boarded-up windows. Half of what lived there the heart thought would kill you. Half of what lived there the heart thought would make you happy. Each of its four chambers has a different postal code, a different key, a different phone ringing through the night. In all cases it's the old-fashioned type with a circular dial, a heavy receiver. If you were to answer, to say hello, you'd hear the only words the heart cares to utter, o love, o love, o love.

HINGE

EASY TO TELL a hawk from a handsaw, but what about a hawk from a hinge? The raptor's wings open and close like hinges that meet on the slim rod of the body; the sky unlocking, then, its blue transparent doors, one after another. The present hinges on the past, the cure on the skill of the physician, the passion on the quality of the kiss. These being proof that a metaphor is a kind of hinge. It makes the mind pivot. Hinge one word to another and see what suddenly swings open, like a gate meant to keep wild horses from the house. *Hyacinth* and *biscuit.* Carl Sandburg says their synthesis is where poetry begins.

ICE

ON A HOT Colombian afternoon as Colonel Aureliano Buendía faced the firing squad, he remembered, in the moment before his death, "that distant afternoon when his father took him to discover ice."

Every few years, the gypsies brought a wonder to the village of Aureliano's childhood: a magnet that yanked pots off kitchen shelves, a telescope that pulled the stars into your eye, false teeth that made twenty years fall from the face of a man, and, in a treasure chest, a slab of ice. Three times Aureliano's father paid the price to place his hand upon it. He said to his son, "This is the greatest invention of our time."

Even the poorest villagers bought a chunk chipped from the slab to suck on. You're sure they said *winter* in a different way after that, licked the warm flesh of their sweethearts more often and more tenderly. The old among them soon discovered that though ice melted in their mouths, the cold inside the body stayed. It frosted the marrow, numbed new possibilities, hardened once-quick rivulets of thought.

If ice is the greatest invention of all time, surely it is death's contrivance. The villagers heard tales of countries north of the equator—places they'd never go—where children turned into wingless swifts and sped far from their homes across glassy lakes, the tibias of horses strapped to their feet with rawhide strips.

IRONING BOARD

1. There's no harm in it, the ironing board. It's pared down
   to bare essentials, simply a level surface with two flat
   feet to stand on. It must be put away after every use. If
   not, things pile up—books, stacks of paper, wet mitts, a
   shirt with buttons missing, milk cartons that need to be
   recycled, nail clippers for a cat. You don't like looking at
   it then, what it says about your life. The ironing board
   remains unflappable. Its purpose is to serve, to stand still,
   to dress itself in whatever you give it: christening gown,
   long-sleeved shirt with cuffs, a demanding skirt with
   pleats. James Joyce said a nun invented barbed wire. The
   same nun invented the ironing board: it takes the sins out
   of clothing, baptizes cloth with steam. One could say it's
   true to its habit and its vow of silence. Under the clothing,
   newly washed, its beak—ironed shut over and over—is
   unable to make a sound.

2. There's nothing more depressing than an ironing board
   set up in a hotel hallway, fourth floor, against the wall.
   It means the patrons are too poor to rent a better room,
   each with its own iron and board, too poor to use the
   hotel's laundry service. Yet like those of higher means,
   they too have their needs for clothing without wrinkles,
   for shiny shoes. Perhaps a job interview, a meeting with
   an old flame not seen in years. The ironing board's cover,
   a slip of once-white cotton over a thin batting, gives you
   goose bumps. You try not to look at it as you pass by. It's
   like the bottom sheet in the room you've booked for two
   nights. Worn-out, soiled with yellow and brown splotches.
   You're sure the mattress underneath is branded with
   burns like the cover of the ironing board, one body on
   top of another, night after night, relentless, pressing their
   heat into the bed.

JELL-O

1. Common on the Canadian prairies, topped with Dream
   Whip or mayonnaise, its colours are so bold it startles
   itself, trembles, fears it's out of place on church basement
   tables bearing platters of sliced turkey, pitchers of gravy,
   bowls of stuffing, potatoes and peas. Anyone unfamiliar
   with it spends a long time trying to figure it out. Animal
   or vegetable? From the ground or the sea? Perhaps a
   Martian staple? Head cheese gone bad? Blood pudding
   with no blood in it? Meant to be eaten with a spoon, like
   most pastry-less desserts, yet there are carrots in this
   batch, and the good women who've cooked the supper
   plop it on their plates next to the meat and gravy. Salt
   Lake City, Utah, claims the highest per capita consump-
   tion in the world. The state has declared Jell-O its official
   snack.

2. Many assume that Jell-O falls into a woman's sphere,
   but it was the builder of the first American steam-
   powered locomotive, Peter Cooper, who filed the patent.
   Pearle B. Wait—another man, though his name sounds

female—bought the rights and developed strawberry, raspberry, orange and lemon flavours. The only Jell-O museum on record is in his hometown, LeRoy, New York, where the main street boasts a Jell-O-brick road.

3. Once, no kitchen pantry was complete without these packets of gelatin, sugar and yummy chemicals that try to taste like fruit. Dame Nellie Melba, the Australian bel canto soprano who sang with Caruso, quipped: "There's only two things I like stiff, and one of them is Jell-O." Now the fanciful concoction is the provenance of the elderly and the sick, poured into huge stainless steel bowls to set in the kitchens of hospitals and care homes. Easy on the digestion, needing no teeth to chew, cheering the dull dinner tray with an otherworldly brightness, it jiggles in the spoon—startled, yes, by its own daring to be food—lifted to the mouth by a shaky hand.

KITCHEN SINK

IF SCIENTIFIC rationalism had a body it would be the
kitchen sink. Turn the right tap, you get cold; the left,
hot. Beyond that, there's little to inscribe in your field
notes. There's the silver spout that curves at the end where
the water pours out. Though *spout* sounds like *snout,* the
former defies comparison. Too inert and inexpressive for
you to write "elephant's trunk"; too impartial to silverfish
for you to propose an anteater's long proboscis. Fridge,
stove, then the sink. They neatly sum up the kitchen. The
sink is the most passive of the three. It confounds, gives
the least back to you, yet it's the one you'll find immor-
talized in a book of idioms: "everything but the kitchen
sink." It plainly refuses to be anything but what it is: the
place where water comes from and where it disappears
when you're done with it. Is there anything more crucial?
Though you're tempted to write "stainless steel oasis," the
kitchen sink is the kitchen sink. Unambiguous, amazing.

KNIFE

A KNIFE is always thirsty. It prefers blood oranges to
apples, rare beef above all else. You could say it has no
gift for the gab. In conversation, it sticks to a point that
never changes. It bores the shine off its sidekicks. Its
straight edge rebukes the roundness of the spoon. Some
say it's not guns that kill, it's people. Those who know
knives insist it's the knife. If there's a carving knife lying
by a platter that swells with a steaming turkey, the most
domestic family man will seize it and hack the bird to
pieces. Borges, who knew the streets of Buenos Aires,
claims the knife is not to blame. Like the scorpion, it can't
change its nature. Some knives are so keenly beautiful
they are passed through generations. You can trace their
history: the thievery and jealous rage, the quick thrust
into the gut and up that spills the viscera of a nation. A
knife owes fealty to no one. A small blade, tucked in a
sleeve, may turn on its owner. Sometimes it inspires great-
ness. Shakespeare ran his tongue along a dagger's cutting
edge and bled a little. Without it, we wouldn't have
Macbeth.

LAMP

OF ALL the rooms in the house, the lamp fancies the
library. On the pages of the open book, it illuminates
invisible cities, the corner of the mind where Iago waits
with a whip of words, the flanks of the wolf hunter's horse
a Blackfoot boy is about to steal in the Cypress Hills. If
there's no library, the lamp prefers the bedroom. It spills
its lumen on a woman's hair, warms the bareness of her
shoulders as she bends toward a mirror to close the clasp
on a string of pearls, each one iridescent, light-licked.
Turned off, the lamp bides its time, waits through the
mornings and the warm afternoons for someone to flick
the switch that manifests the first *let there be*. Because it
lives indoors, it has a nostalgia for the days when lamp-
lighters attended to the tall lanterns in the streets, the
snow falling, the yellow pools cast by the burning oil
more beautiful for all the dark and cold around them.
Then, anyone out walking could see the lamps light up
in the sky high above, on every planet in the galaxy a
woman fastening a string of tiny moons around her neck;
on every star, someone reading.

LIGHT BULB

AT FIRST you thought you'd plant it with the rest. But
you were defeated by its fragility and the stem's refusal to
grow. The bulb turned out to be insensitive to spring and,
though half its name was light, sunshine meant nothing to
it. Glass made it glimmer like a living thing, but you soon
discovered it was not. Why call the object *bulb,* then? Why
give it that shape? Isn't this false advertising, the height
of corporate deceit, igniting our hopes that it will be a
brighter daffodil, a tulip for the dark, a gleaming gladi-
olus, its tall stalk like a string of old-fashioned Christmas
lights turning on its blossoms one by one?

LINOLEUM

YOU DIDN'T know you loved linoleum, hard under the heel, especially the red and patterned kind—its vain attempt to be a thousand knotted Persian threads. It never gave up trying—you admire that—though the feet knew the difference and the knees, when you used it for a prayer rug. Superstitious as a child, you swore off treats so your pleading would work—chocolates, the little Avon lipstick samples, candy cigarettes. You gave them up, but it didn't pay off; your father came home drunk, the sick dog died. You didn't know you loved linoleum until last week, when your friend showed you the attic in the house she'd just moved into. There was no insulation, the single window didn't open, you could hardly breathe from the heat. But hundred-year-old rafters rose from the floor to the underside of the roof, beautiful and bare, and in the centre gleamed a looks-like-new sheet of red linoleum printed with fat, straw-coloured flowers, waiting for someone from the fifties to build a room around it, waiting for a child to steal in and kneel on its amiably unforgiving surface in the dead of night.

LOBE

COY WATTLE at the bottom of the ear, it has nothing
to do with the workings of the inner canal, the stirrup,
hammer and anvil in their twenty-four-hour shifts. In fact,
it has no job. The size of a weasel's nose, but it cannot
smell. Larger than the ear of a mouse, but it cannot hear.
It is a small nothingness, an afterthought, a left-over bit
pinched to the auricular like a smidgen of dough flattened
by a baker's thumb. Its only purpose is to be delectable.
Even on the ear of a man, it is a plush exposed clitoris
made lusciously to fit the tip of a tongue.

MEASURE

A WEIGHT of thirty stone. A horse five hands high. A
thousand-li-long road that starts with the first step. The
magnitude of zero between two primes. The span of the
Bridge of Sighs. Dante's nine circles, their diameters and
the leagues of suffering that lie between. The math of
miracles: Jesus healed ten lepers; subtract nine; only one
returned to thank him. The number of wheat fields wind
travels in its lifetime. The yardstick hanging from a nail
by the door frame, where your mother drew a line and
pencilled in your height. Sin's wages, twenty paces, the
thinning of a wedding band over fifty years. (Where does
the lost gold go?) An inchworm. The exact degree of cold
that ruins a friendship. The distance the dark one travels
to meet you in the marketplace at Samarra. The miles to
go before the little horse can sleep.

THE MIDNIGHT NEWS

EVERYWHERE AND nowhere an old rain is falling.
It stinks of mud from the trenches and animals in too-
close quarters in the ark.

A small war hasn't ended.

The second greatest story ever told was told, and you
missed it.

Scientists in Belgium confirm there's no kindness left in
the world. One hundred percent of people won't stop to
assist a fallen man crying out for help. Dogs, even golden
retrievers, won't turn toward him or tug on their leashes
as they walk past.

In Salzburg the newborn babies are covered in horse
blood.

Bicycles have stopped. They've turned into exercise bikes,
some with small computers attached to the handlebars
to clock the distance the rider isn't travelling. Tour de
France officials are working through the night to change

the rules of the race, which begins next week. Commuters, bound for work, are spinning in their driveways; children are stuck in the schoolyards, pedalling for all they're worth. In a statement released today, the mayor of London claims this started as a curse on couriers in rush-hour traffic. He warns the phenomenon could shut his city down.

Greenland reports that the ice that hasn't melted is turning black.

The ghosts of larks baked in pies in Paris are batting into the heads of sleepers. Insomnia is plaguing the city.

On the universal clock, seven years have passed. All the cells in your body have just died.

Cockroaches mate for life.

There's too much sadness in inner-city rooms, even if there's a small balcony for a barbecue.

Here's what's up next. We'll go to Jerusalem, where a suicide bomber has turned herself over to the authorities. She is nine months pregnant, they are afraid to touch her, she stands at the end of everything, it could be ashes falling around her, it could be snow.

MIRROR

A MIRROR is a pond that hardened into ice and moved inside. The frame around it stops its melt. Weary of gazing at the sky, it needed something else to look at, something that looked back. For this, it sets a blank expression; it never interrupts or shivers or allows its desires to dart like silver minnows across a face. However, in the world of the house, it is dying of boredom and regret. It longs to see a damselfly, to taste the rain, to feel the weight of water lilies as the buds thicken with the imperative to bloom. Servant to the occupants, the mirror is dying of holding everything inside. Like Cassandra, it's been granted the ruthless grace of accuracy, though it must appear undiscerning, unable to separate the beauty from the ugliness in ordinary life. Though more attention is paid to it than any other object in the room, it is strangely invisible. People stare into it several times a day with deepening attention, noting bristles on a chin, a tremor in the upper lip, the eyes' dissemblance. They never see the mirror.

MOON

A PAUCITY of rhymes but so many metaphors, most worn
thin. A wheel of cheese, a snow-blind eye, the old moon in
the young moon's arms. You wish Christy Moore would
write a song about that old one. Surely it's not true to say
it watches or follows us across the countryside, though
you'd swear that happens. And though you've never seen
anyone grow fur and howl, the moon does stir things up.
When it's bright enough, it casts our shadows in the night.
They're let out after dark so rarely they make the most of
it, sometimes leading you the wrong way home. That's
when, if you're lucky, you'll see the white hares dancing
in the snow, the moon with its mouth wide open as if in
wonder—can you say that just this once?—as if in wonder,
the world luminous with winter, the wild hares leaping.

MOP

THE MOP lacks the mystery of the broom. No one thinks
of it steering through the stars. No one assumes it has
a living name. Also, it lacks the broom's sleek lines, its
held-togetherness. A mop is a floppy thing. If you were
unkind, you'd call it homely. On the other hand, its
syntax is to be admired. It's so simple, requiring only
"and" and an adverb or two to move it "back and forth"
or "up and down" or "over and over and over." Of course
it has a head, fat worms of cotton or some synthetic, but
does anyone assume the mop is thinking? It's best it
doesn't. More than the broom, it does its work in places
of great mess and consequence: the slaughter house,
the hospital, kitchens where bottles have been thrown
against a wall, pots full of sauces dumped from the stove,
someone crying in a corner far into the night. Mop it up.

What you can. Sometimes sounds get tangled in the
long absorbent strings—when you wring them out, you
hear what children hear when they shout or scream
underwater. There are no mops in the Book of Revelation,
yet they have a long history, and their future is assured.
At Culloden, at the Somme, at Vadencourt, old women
no one pays attention to push their mops back and forth
across the battlefields, keeping the new grass clean.

MOUTH

DOES IT need to be said? The mouth is the most
obnoxious part of the body. It leaps between Cicero
and gibberish, drools when you fall asleep in public
places. Blah, blah, blah, it says, and you want to disown
it, but then it throws a kiss and a stranger, walking dully
along, feels a smack of happiness land on his cheek.
The mouth is unfamiliar with manners, with common
sense or cool reflection. Just for kicks it bullies the belly.
Taunts it with deprivation—the belly growls—then stuffs
it like a Butterball meant to feed a family of fifteen.

Every day, no matter what your plans, the mouth plots
a raid on the inarticulate, opening and closing its gate
of teeth, tensing its tongue. The brain plays tricks on it:
logorrhoea, Tourette's, baby talk to grownups. So easy,
when the finger points at pictures, to become a lamb, a
pig, a duck. While a tooth fears a doorknob, the thumb
a mousetrap, the mouth fears a mime, the lethal conse-
quence of those never-moving lips.

You list its pleasures—ice cubes, nipples, raspberries,
et cetera, the spicy and the sweet—but there's something
more essential, what too often as time passes it must
learn to live without: its favourite thing—the taste of
another mouth.

NAVEL

A MAN-SIZED, deeply whorled thumb made a dip there as in dough; the tied-off end of a broken balloon drifted down and landed in that place. Navel gazer, we say, meaning something negative, a person who can't see past herself. But why don't we obsess, why don't we think about this gnomic rune more often? Mysterious as the paw print of a snow leopard in a mountain drift, as ordinary as a pit inside a peach, as far away from function now as an extra feline toe, could it be a blind third eye sunk into the fat? Whatever else, it's the final remnant of the snaky cord that attached us like an astronaut to the mother ship. There are mornings we feel the tug. Try as we may, we can't recall that cut, though sometimes we wake with a start, floating in the darkness of the outer world, irreparably alone.

NEEDLE

KEROSENE CASTS the best light for threading, your
grandmother said. Some days for no reason she could
ascertain, the eye accepted only black, and she'd change
her plans for what she'd mend. She was the one who told
you about the rich man and the camel. A camel could
get through the eye of a needle; a rich man couldn't. You
weren't sure what that meant, but it sounded like another
bad excuse for being poor. You'd never seen a camel, or a
rich man for that matter, though some owned more land
than others and your dad had lost the farm. The other
kind of needle left a scar on your arm so that you wouldn't
get smallpox. You were a baby then. In grade one, you
lined up two by two with the other children, all of you
inching down the long hallway to the door of the nurse's
room. Several fainted before they got their vaccinations,
fear running down the line as if through a vein. By high
school you'd heard the phrase "shoot up." It was three
more years before you knew someone who did it. You
found the needle beside a Mars bar wrapper on the floor

of your car after your friend had borrowed it for the night.
You picked it up by the plunger, holding the point away
from you as if it were the tail of a scorpion about to strike.
You felt stupid. Your friend said he wore nothing but
long sleeves because sunlight gave him hives. Until then,
"tracks" meant the place your grandmother took you to
wave at the man at the back of the caboose as the train
roared through the crossing. Most times he waved back.

NO

SUCH A small word, packing so much punch. When used
alone, it flummoxes linguists. It's not an interjection or
an adverb, certainly not the name of any person, place or
thing. Some call it and its opposite grammatical particles,
which brings to mind physics and collisions, *yes* and *no*
banging together inside a reactor and *maybe* tumbling
out. Usually it's not welcome around the house, particu-
larly in the bedroom or when chores are divvied up. It
can be the catalyst of many a shouting match. Be careful
what you say no to. Too much of it dulls your taste buds,
terminates temerity, turns off the lights in the pleasure
centre of your brain. Imagine it replacing the last words
of Molly Bloom! Several languages, including Latin and
Chinese, don't have a word for *no*. Poets say it less often
than others in any mother tongue. Take Pablo Neruda. In
his *Odas elementales* he embraces everything: mohair socks,
watermelons, the hidden kindness of firemen, the birds of
Chile, the panther, the lemon, a rooster in yellow boots,
the storms of Córdoba, sadness and wine—on his beloved
seashore, his mouth full of salt and yes.

NOSE

THE NOSE wishes it had been raised by wolves. Or even by farm dogs, who can sniff out a rat in a stack of bales as high as a house. What envy your nose feels for the blind old mutt who smelled his master, Odysseus, through his disguise, though everyone else was tricked. Even the famous honkers of Bob Hope, Jimmy Durante, Cyrano de Bergerac pick up a fraction of what canine noses will inhale in the animals' short lives. For you, there are things that compensate: bacon spitting in a pan, rubber boots, sunlight on your forearm, that secret spot behind a child's ear, a horse's forehead, mitts on radiators, the breath of your dog that wakes your nostrils in the morning when he licks your cheek.

NOSE: A STORY

WHEN THE wolf boy was captured in the woods outside
Paris and taken to King Louis' court, he couldn't stand
the stench. He covered his face with a bandana, like the
robber of a stage coach, until his nose lost some of its
wolfish sensitivity. But even after years had passed and he
could read the Bible and dress like a minion in foppery
and shoes, his nose couldn't stop coursing the air, flaring
its nostrils when a woman entered the room, sometimes
going so far as to bury itself in her bare shoulders or
nuzzle her breasts if they blurted above the neckline. He
met his wife this way. The smell of her never failed to
make him drool.

One of their sons became the rose gardener at
Versailles, then the owner of a small *parfumerie*. When
the fragrances overwhelmed him, he abandoned the
trade and disappeared. Some claimed he'd been spotted
floating on a raft off the rocks of Gibraltar, where the
scents were few and those that reached him had been
wrung out by the wind.

The second son became a baker of country breads in Bordeaux. His customers lined up every morning before he raised the blinds, opened the door and let them in. Except for the waste, he'd have driven them away. All he needed in his life were the smells that wafted from the loaves as they turned gold above the burning wood, then cooled on the shelves beneath the window. He never left his shop but slept on a rug near the ovens, dough rising on the counters in the dark that would soon be 3:00 AM, the hour of suicides and insomniacs, the holy hour at which begins the baking of our daily bread.

OBJECTS

IF THERE'S a God-of-the-Gaps, used to explain what science can't, there must be a God-of-Objects. There's something about objects that intrigues. If you gaze at one—a wrench, a cheese grater, a paper clip—with rapt attention, after twenty minutes you'll be worn out and have to take a nap. Czesław Miłosz published an anthology called *A Book of Luminous Things*. William Matthews said if an object fails to interest us, it's not its fault but our own. As proof, he offered, "How easily happiness begins by / dicing onions." Francis Ponge exclaimed, "O infinite resources of the thickness of things."

We try to diminish their clout by calling them stuff and clutter. But so much, we know, depends upon a wheelbarrow, an elastic band, a toothpick, a jar in Tennessee. The God-of-Objects, cousin to the God-of-the-Gaps, can be sensed sometimes, a solid otherness that makes us shiver, a there-ness that defies comparison, an almost hidden radiance that refuses to be ignored, though we ignore it every day. Someone's father dies and leaves a drawer of ballpoint pens. Someone keeps the bowl in which her mother kneaded bread dough, a big white bowl too heavy for her to lift from the upper cupboard shelf.

Things outlast us, even the fragile—an Etruscan pitcher, a thousand-year-old piece of glass from the Tang Dynasty, Trotsky's spectacles, which fell to his desk and cracked when the climbing axe struck the back of his head. Soon enough we'll join the ranks of what endures— ashes scraped into a plastic sack or a mute articulation of many bones.

PLATE

IF THE MOON could be sliced thinly as a radish, it would
be this plate. Bone china, white with blue in it, the colour
carrying that particular from the purest fire. No saucer or
platter can hold its own beside it. You'd have to divorce
a husband who chipped it, send a child to live with his
grandmother in the forest. Surely the moon is lesser for
it, and you are more. You wash it by hand, you polish it
with silk. You tell no one you breathe on it and wipe your
breath away. You'd like to save it for a cake, angel food
with an icing of meringue and coconut, barely toasted.
You'd like to dine from it on the Himalayas' highest peak
in falling snow. Still, you respect its use, its daily function,
set it on the table for the one who's always late for supper.
After you've gone to bed, in the darkness of the dining
room, the plate begins to glow on the good white cloth,
its pull an anti-gravity that keeps the one who's missing
from the door.

QUICKSILVER

WINTER SO bitter that year, the thermometer shattered. Careful with the shards of glass, you scooped up the tiny rivulet that looked like liquid from Polaris and let it pool in your hand. It seemed more alive than many living things. It shook and quivered. If you touched it with your tongue, would your words gleam bright before they tarnished? If you dipped your fingers, would you have a lesser Midas touch? This was long before the spill at Minamata, before the Cree in Manitoba fell sick from eating fish. When you were young, it was one of the few gifts the cold of your country gave you. *Quicksilver,* kin of ice and ether, the name itself like something from a fairytale, a trembling wishing pearl inside a fish's belly, a coin-like puddle you split in two and placed on each eyelid so you could navigate the night ahead, your sight lit up with neon.

RADIATOR

UP AGAINST the wall, the bellows of an accordion,
petrified. After céilidhs in countless parish halls, rumpus
rooms and kitchens, it can't be silenced. While you try to
sleep, it squeezes out a loud metallic music. How brave
it is, how willing to go off on its own without a fiddle to
accompany it, without a woman's lap to rest in, without
the bletherin' wail of whiskey to wake the newly dead.

RAKE

THE FIRST rake was a hand. The older the better, rachitic
fingers permanently bent, a scraping tool of bone and
flesh. The aged, then, had a purpose and were not parted
from the rest. They could kneel for hours, moving slowly
forward like penitents approaching a terracotta god,
clearing the surface, scraping parallel runnels for seeds,
singing a raking song as they sang a song for scything
and for grinding grain. The next rake was a branch with
the right configuration of twigs. A boy had watched a
crow use a tool, and so he made one, too. The old grew
wary. This was centuries ago. No one mentions the impor-
tance of the *Corvus* in the history of the rake or the exile
of the aged. Now the garden rake is a wooden handle
attached to an upper row of iron teeth from a jaw as big
as a crocodile's. Harmless, really, that half bite, though it
makes a music of lost sounds as it scores the earth.

SCISSORS

TOO LITERAL, too practical for your needs. You want
them to cut away grief, to shred into ribbons the hooded
cloak of aging draped over your shoulders, heavier with
each passing year. They were at their most magical with
Matisse, when he shook too much to paint. Think of
*La Gerbe, Blue Nude with Hair in the Wind, La Perruche et
la Sirène*. They are magical now when they sculpt a sheet
of paper into a snowflake, especially since you live so
far from winter's dazzle. How you wish they could scissor
a blue shadow from a snowdrift for you to tuck into your
pocket. From the brilliant air, how you wish their blades
could separate and snip the warm mist of your breath
for you to carry into whatever cold awaits you in the days
to come.

SCREW

MORE HOLD-FAST than the nail but less adaptable to what's at hand, the screw won't be put in place by a field-stone or the heel of a boot. It's a small triumph of precision, a panegyric to the particular. The watchmaker needs a special screwdriver; so does the sewing-machine repair man, the clockmaker, the undertaker, the orthopaedic surgeon who fastens bone to metal and bone to bone. It's hard to believe this common doodad could be so essential. Lobsters live without it; so does grass. But then there are eyeglasses, automotive assembly lines, the oven door, the microscope, Big Ben, the Eiffel Tower, the engine rooms of cruise ships. What holds a family together, secures a woman to her past, lets the door to the future swing open and shut? The screw has a noble history. Archimedes, born in 287 BC, is its father. You wonder what he'd make of "Screw you." Really, that rude curse is inaccurate. In the coital act there's no spiralling, no incremental twists.

Rather, the penis, threadless along its length and pointless at the business end, rams in head first. Archimedes, pumping gloriously into his wife, may have shouted "Huerēka" (I found it!) when he came, but his joyful genital gadgetry did not give him the inspiration for the screw.

SHAKERS

1. As compact and canny as a bomb, the salt shaker made
   of glass takes its rightful place at the table. You could slip
   it in your pocket and feel dangerous, let it settle beside
   a book of matches from the Baudelaire Hotel. When it's
   by your plate in the early morning it makes you think
   of snow settling inside a globe, of the half light of grainy
   photographs, of stars ground with a pestle. It makes
   you think of pure idea. It's a perfect paradox of energy
   and calmness, of modesty and conceit. It's what you'd
   place beside a candle at an altar. Though humourless,
   it makes you question why you always trust there's salt
   inside it. The small holes on top are what you'd punch in
   a container that holds an animal, so it could breathe.

2. The spice inside the pepper shaker wasn't mined in
   caverns where men die daily, or dragged from the wild
   waters of the sea. The berries from trees lined up in rows
   on some plantation, dried and ground, make this shaker
   seem less prone to speculation or surprise. Still, what we
   see through the glass could be crushed cinders from a
   railroad track or gritty pollen the shadows of graveyard
   trees scatter in the wind. The shaker's constant presence
   at the table shows the tongue's desire to become a martyr,
   to translate a flame. It's an hourglass without a waist,
   measuring, with grains of midnight, the little time we
   have left to eat.

SHOE

THE SHOE the old dog dropped on the step at dusk. Last
week it was a dead cat, and all night you worried that he'd
killed it. He's always liked cats, but his mind is slipping.
Some mornings you have to remind him it's time to eat.
He's a brown Lab grown grey around the muzzle. His
right hip shows signs of dysplasia. At least suspecting him
of murder is not an issue when the victim is a shoe.

It's a man's left shoe, black, with a built-up sole, as if
the owner is a 1950s' child of polio. Perhaps he's not lame,
just short, and the partner of this shoe is also heightened.
It resembles an army boot with the top sliced off, the
leather sole swollen in sympathy for the foot infected in
the trenches. You can't imagine anyone in town this might
belong to. Should you put up a sign in the post office?
You slip your own foot into it, think "walk a mile," et
cetera. You clump down the hall, feeling like a fool, the
dog barking without getting up. Your new gait makes you
so ungainly you feel you've found a new kind of grace.

Even though it's bad luck to leave a shoe on a table,
you put the shoe on the table—it looks quite comfy there,
though unlikely—then open the door to let the dog out.
"Time to pee," you say, and watch him trudge, one hip
lower than the other, across the yard. You try to remember
how old he is. Two hours later he's not home, dark has
fallen, and you're waiting for the other shoe to drop.

SHOVEL

THE SHOVEL exhausted all forms of being before settling into this one. Its character is clear. It defies cleanliness and shine. In every country, in every century, it performs the elemental rite of all humanity. Turns the soil for planting: potatoes, corn, the body of a cat, a child, a woman. There is no monotony in this. Long ago it lost its grip on time. You'd swear it is a noun but it's a verb, in stasis, waiting in the shed for a shift in circumstance or season. Winter, the ground frozen three feet down, gives the shovel many hours to call up from its past the roots of words. *Weary* once meant to plod through mud. *Hussy* meant a country wife, who would have been handy with any outdoor tool. Though the shovel is used to cover up, it never falsifies. Nor does it show charity: made for hand and foot, it bends the back, stiffens the muscles of legs and arms, blisters. In a garden of graves, the shovel is sorrow's tool. Its soul is iron and wood. No matter how long its exile from the dig, there is the good earth, waiting.

SKY

THE SKY is a blouse snatched from the back of a woman.
No. The sky is a muddle of clouds that won't sit still in
the lecture hall. No, the sky's soaked with sweat, and
the rain won't wring it out. The sky's an open brawl, a
boom of mirrors, the roof blowing in. No, the sky is the
blouse ripped from the back of a woman rolled in a ditch.
Blue blouse, half silk, half cotton, buttons torn off. No.
Mullioned with a million windows, the sky is a warehouse
that stores the archives of the light. No, the sky is the sky.
And it's world-weary, like love worn out.

SNAIL

IT SAILS without sails in the garden, so slow, if it were
a ship, there'd be no wind. Enough has been said about
the house it carries on its back. You're charmed by its
eyes on stilts, little periscopes of sight it can pull into its
soft body. Its slime is a gift, a viscous track laid under its
belly. The snail's not made of blubber but it looks like fat
trimmed from a pork chop, or a dollop of lard squeezed
from a pastry tube. You could go on about its constitu-
tion—it's still moving past—but you've yet to speak about
the horns that rival its eyes for the pleasure they give you.
Not meant for fighting, without points or velvet, they tap
the air as delicately as the buds of fingers touching the
inner walls of the womb. And they glisten, as if licked by
something as small as a chickadee's tongue.

SNOW

HOW MUCH snow and grief have in common: their
connection with the seasons, their silence, their slow
accumulation. Consider the woman who, sensing the
hush of the first snowfall, gets out of bed in the early light
of morning and lifts a man's loafers from the back of the
closet. Pulls on her boots and parka and steps outside.
Placing her hands inside his shoes, she bends, plants his
footprints next to her own, straightens, takes another
step and does the same thing again and again, all the way
from the porch to the garden gate. There she stops and
looks back, his tracks beside hers—she has matched the
drag of one heel and the longer stride—the snow briefly
holds them, then, impeccably falling, fills them in.

SPOONS

OF THE utensils, spoons have the deepest reach into the past. They remember being liquid, silver or steel. That's why, if your hand is steady, they can carry any kind of broth to your lips without a spill. They come closer than the others to human anatomy, the palm cupped to lift mouthfuls of water from a stream. When coupled, there is music in spoons, their clatter as pagan and lustful as the drumming of a ruffed grouse. If they have a flaw, it's their love of rhyme, their choices so limited they've turned the moon into a cliché.

A baby is safe alone with spoons. They have never entertained a murderous thought. Their favourite substance is pudding, thin or thick; their favourite temperatures the two extremes. A single spoon on the table beside a shallow bowl means someone very old is about to eat.

STONE

A STONE is a clock whose face you can't read. There's too
much time in it. It keeps to itself, elbows close to the body,
legs tucked in. Sometimes turtles are mistaken for stones,
but stones move eons more slowly and have no need of
water, though water pleases them when it falls. Rain
clarifies, makes confident each colour, turns their greys
thundercloud blue. Since the eggs that stones lay are
imaginary, stones determine what's inside the shells. In
one, a tool box with a rusted chisel. In others, a hurricane,
a Geiger counter, an epitaph.

STOOL

THE STOOL was irrefutably itself, solid and without
pomp. Three-legged, short, made of wood. Confrere of
the cow. Music to its ears was milk needling the sides of a
pail. The cry of barn cats. The boots of the farmer crack-
ling through the sweet, dry straw. It was hardy, it was
Thomas Hardy, it was essential to what happened next:
cream, cheese, pale butter and the nursing of babies when
they were weaned.

Then its name appeared in the dictionary as a synonym
for excrement.

Mammal, mainly human.

It lost its self-confidence. Its balance.

You'll notice now it's rare. Across the country, dairy
barns hum with big machines. No need for something
to sit on, to give the milker the right height and angle
to lean into the cow's warm flank and reach under. No
hands pulling the teats. The animals are so confined, so
crammed together, the smell is overpowering.

The smell of stool.

STOVE

THE STOVE has a quiet purposefulness, sure of its
responsibilities to family life. It's impervious to pain, the
burn of its own heat, the wounds pans leave on Arborite
and wood. Immobility made manifest, it's scrupulously
detached from the goings-on in the kitchen, the quarrels
and embraces, the dog gnawing a strip of rawhide, the
necessary screw that rolls under it and will never be found
again. Unlike the fridge, the stove does much of its work
in the open, but it's more hazardous. The plug at the end
of its cord is the biggest in the house. At its centre lies
the hearth, its powers intact, though no one gathers there
for singalongs or comfort from the night. More than the
setting of clocks, turning the knobs on the stove teaches
you precision and the perils of the mind's slippage. The
smallest click, the tiny difference between "On" and "Off,"
can mean a Feast of Mercy or the house and all who dwell
there devoured by fire.

TABLE

IN MOST of the paintings it is covered by a thick white cloth so the artist can demonstrate his mastery with drapery, its sheen and shadows. The host is seated at the centre, six disciples on either side. A carpenter's son, he has noted the joints, the dovetail, the mortise and tenon, the legs planed into sturdy slimness and, under the cloth, the smoothness and colour drawn from the planks by hours of sanding and the rubbing in of oils. The table bears the weight of platters heaped with food, slabs of lamb and roasted chickens, unleavened bread that hasn't yet become a body. You can't help but think a table is a good use of a tree. To build it, a carpenter need not feel ashamed of pounding nails into wood. And no one sitting at it is thirsty or forsaken. There is ample room for a multitude of jugs. In the grain of the wood you can read the table's past, the years of drought and rain, the wood-worm infestation, but nothing in it shows what's about to happen: nothing reveals this is the last table at which the host will eat. Or that wine, which now stains the beard and lips of the one who will betray him, will soon become His blood.

TOASTER

UNLIKE THE mousetrap, perfect from the outset in
form and function, the toaster has changed. There used
to be two small doors hinged at the bottom. You swung
them down, laid the bread upon them, then clicked
them shut. Halfway through, you opened them again
and flipped the slices to brown the other sides. This took
skill. Many breakfast makers burned their fingers. Early
doorless models simplified the task, though they some-
times popped the toast a foot above the grills. You had to
remain at your toasting station, alert and quick, to snatch
the finished product from the air. It took years of observa-
tion in toaster labs for someone to tweak the math and
double the slices. The other change is more significant.
The slots have widened. This redesign takes in the bagel,
the scone, the croissant, the English muffin, the kaiser
bun. What's missing? A slot thin enough to toast pitas,
thinner still for tortillas. Blessed is the country that would
fund the creation of such an amenable machine and then
deliver it to every household in the land.

TOOTH

THE PART of the body closest to a tree is the tooth, the
deep roots of it. If you don't believe me, wait till you get a
molar pulled; the hole in the gum will remind you of the
hole left where you dug the poplar out. For years, without
taste buds—and therefore no reward—the tooth chewed
and chewed. Now it's the miniature of a tree stump turned
to ivory. You'd swear that it's centuries older than the rest
of you, that someone found it sunk in permafrost beside a
tiny Dorset carving of a swan.

TOWEL

THE RUB and thick of it, the fabric (if you're in luck)
abrasive as a cat's lick, a gardener's chapped hands.
Nothing knows the body better. Wrinkles or not, folds
of fat or bones erupting. The towel's task is to soak it up.
From babyhood to old woman, old man, it travels the
territory of the skin from face to feet, the parts in shadow
and the parts in light. Blind in its touch, its roughness
intimate, often it's mistaken for a paramour, a husband
of long standing, a good wife. Towel—do we make too
much of it? Or should it be in line for sainthood of the
domestic kind? Cast out with no redress, thin by then
from many washes, in the bin of the rag seller, rarely does
it smell of flowers.

UMBRELLA

1. Also called brolly and bumbershoot, parasol when the offending ephemera that falls is light. You like the French, *parapluie,* regret the German, *Regenschirm,* admire most things Italian, the language from which *umbrella* comes. Whatever it's called, whatever its country of origin, in a past life the umbrella must have harmed the wind—the wind, without doubt, plots its undoing. Flips it inside out, snaps its ribs, clatters it over stones. The British nanny Mary Poppins made the best of wind's revenge, but you know her story isn't true.

2. To open an umbrella inside a house will bring bad luck. To close it in the middle of a bridge will lead to a wrong decision. To put an umbrella into its stand when it is drenched will bring a week of tears. Crows believe umbrellas are their rivals. They drop pebbles and splat them with rivulets of shit. If you see three crows together, it could be murder. Don't meet their gaze, look as casual as you can, close your umbrella and risk the rain.

3. Red and yellow umbrellas bring joy to the viewer, especially when seen from the thirty-second floor of a hotel. Lucky is the old woman who believes she holds a blossom on a rigid stem. Crowds part for her even in the meanest cities, and the wind lets her be.

4. *Up* is the umbrella's favourite word. It insists on being on top, as high above the sidewalk as the arm and handle will allow. Really, what keeps you dry is not the cloth stretched between the spokes but the absence it creates, the want of weather around your head and shoulders. If you stay too long within the umbrella's temperate zone, its arid emptiness, your thirst will become intolerable. You'll have too little spit to swallow, and though you're sometimes sadder than the rain, no tears will fall.

5. Only a Chinese fan or the squeezebox of an accordion folds up so neatly. Wait a minute... what about a nesting crane, its spindly legs tucked beneath its breast, its neck stretched along its back when it is sleeping? What about the snow? Thousands of flakes falling one on top of another, forming a drift—hard, compact—and underneath, the ground stays dry.

6. The umbrella of the jellyfish is not an accoutrement that offers shelter. It is the entire creature, a fringed dome more beautiful than any cathedral's, limber, fluxed, more see-through than a window and gleaming with a light as curious as the firefly's. A shock to your fingertip—what is its matter, both watery and tough?—it came into the world long before the word *umbrella*. It must be an orphan of the rain. It must be the ocean's sacring bell that rings in the harbours without a sound.

VACUUM

NATURE ABHORS a vacuum. So do writers if a page
remains blank too long or the pressure seeps out of a
story; so do sentimentalists if the heart stays empty, and
cats if the vacuum has wheels and a long hose that sucks
up hairballs. What to make of that double *u,* as if the
word itself has suction enough to pull in an extra under-
the-bed, among-the-dust-bunnies vowel.

VAGINA

SURELY A MAN with one thing on his mind came up
with *vagina,* Latin for *scabbard* or *sheathe.* It's difficult
to know what to call it. Its oldest synonym is the vilest
curse. You find solace in translations from the Chinese:
Pillow of Musk, Inner Heart, Jade Gate. "The joints of thy
thighs are like jewels," King Solomon sang in Hebrew,
then praised what he called the navel, "like a rounded
goblet, which never lacks blended wine." Often it's named
without naming. In a letter to Joséphine, Napoleon wrote,
"I kiss your heart, and then a little lower, and then much
lower still." What it most resembles is not a cat but a
flower, unfolding on an O'Keeffe canvas, petals wet with
light. Or, minus the stinging tentacles, a sea anemone, an
ocean-dweller that doesn't smell like fish. All tuck and
salty muscle, it's mysterious, even to a woman. Doorway
of Life, Lotus Boat, the Deep One. You worked through
the dirty jokes and schoolyard taunts to learn it's cleaner

than a mouth, you can't lose anything inside it, and it's never grown teeth. Home from battle, when Napoleon kissed Joséphine's much-lower-still, ululations streamed down the palace hallways. Maids smiled in sweet anticipation of the night ahead. Others pressed their knees together, prayed the Virgin Mary would stop their ears. The Double-Lipped, the Beautiful, Quim.

WARTS

WORSE THAN pimples, warts go deeper, back to words
like *weal* and *wen* and *witch*. There's something satisfying
about squeezing a zit, but nothing comes out of a wart.
There's no injury you can inflict upon it. Pain foreshadows
a pimple; you know exactly where a red bump will appear
by morning. A wart comes out of nowhere, and you've
done nothing to deserve it: it's not your period, you
haven't eaten too much chocolate or poutine. Warts origi-
nate on another planet, where everything is dry, prehis-
toric and inexplicable. A planet where toads are king and
warts a sign of their tenacity. But you're stuck with here,
a sky with one moon that seems to draw warts out of you.
If a doctor burns them off, they come back. You've heard
you can sell them for a nickel, but who's the buyer? The
Irish rub them with a piece of raw meat, then bury the

meat in a field at night. By morning, they say, the warts
will be gone. The terrestrial common toad wears his warts
well. Kiss the one in the thicket on his horny forehead and
see what happens next. If he's lucky he'll remain a toad,
the brown pearls erupting on his skin as beautiful to his
Bufo wife as the throaty tremolos of his song.

WASHING MACHINE—
NEW, FRONT-LOADING

SO MANY knobs and buttons and beeping sounds, it's
possible the machine rockets the laundry into outer space
to get it clean. Once you shut the round door and hear
the sound of water, you can't open it. It's locked like the
windows of a spaceship or a submarine. Nothing to do
but leave the basement and return an hour later. The wet
clothes in the tub have never looked so weary, so relieved
to see you. This may be why they stay clean longer, why
more of them spill from the basket when you walk down
the stairs to load the machine. The socks, so good at
getting lost, get lost more often. You can't stop thinking
of the word *abduction*. You begin to stand back, toss in
the clothes from some distance. What used to be the most
tedious of tasks makes you tense with anticipation. There
are blocks of time you can't remember. The glass door of
the machine stares like the mutant eye of a giant cyclop-
idian fish. Reflected in its glare, in the pause between
rinse and spin, the basement pulses with a strange,
inhuman light.

WATER

1. Crucial to the house, found in kitchens, bath and laundry rooms; outside, it's piped to the pond and to faucets where hoses sip and swallow. Charmed by summer, they coil or stretch across the yard, the sun warming their long, glabrous backs.

2. Once the world was water. Now it's drying up: the aquifers, the great lakes, the rivers birthed by glaciers, the glaciers too. Rain won't be enough. Hope won't be enough. But humans, after all, are mostly made of water. Those desperate ones harvested for organs will soon be drained. The rich in their glass houses will drink the poor, beautifully bottled, some with sparkle and fizz, others regrettably flat.

WHEELBARROW

YES, SO MUCH depends: the garden, the variable foot, the woman who carries in her arms less and less each year. The barrow balances on its one wheel as gracefully as a flamingo on his pink leg. It accepts the garden's narrowing paths, overgrown with vines and bushes that need cutting back. It accepts the slower step, the arthritic hip, the glaze of rain, the absence of white chickens. The two handles, like the handlebars of a bike, shift with the weight and bend of whatever body sets it in motion. It accepts the stooped back, the breathlessness, the mire of mud. One wheelbarrow can outlast a life and, in some cases, feel more useful. Though it seems commonplace when it's at rest, the woman who guides it from the shed knows the fortitude and beauty of its nature. Past the late summer flowers to the vegetable patch she coaxes the wheelbarrow with the names her grandmother gave it: *my wooden ox, my gliding horse.*

X MARKS the spot, but there are few around the house,
unless you own a game of jacks or collect old dolls, the
homemade kind, with cross-stitches for eyes. You can find
X as well on labels glued to jars of poison stored under the
sink and in the garden shed, the letter made of femurs and
placed below a skull. *X*'s Phoenician ancestor, samekh,
means fish. Even to this day, there's something fishy about
X. You remember it drawn on the blackboard in school,
the teacher saying, "*X* is the unknown." You couldn't stop
thinking it could be chalked across everything outside
the self—the cat, the red-eared turtle in the pond, clouds
and sumac, a good night's sleep, yeast blooming in sugar
water in a measuring cup. The last entry in *Webster's* under
X is *xyster.* You'd be suspicious if you found it with the
can opener, whisk, meat thermometer and garlic crusher
in your drawer of kitchen gadgets. Used in surgery, and
from the Greek, it's an instrument for scraping bones.

YO-YO

MEANING A stupid person, meaning brilliance on the
cello, meaning the world's second-oldest toy (a doll was
the first), a flattened spool with a deep groove in the
centre. Coiled around it was a long string with a slipknot
tied at the end. You slipped your index finger through
the small loop and spun the spool up and down as the
string unwound and wound again. You did this for hours,
walking home alone when the teacher made you stay after
school; on the weekends standing between the lilacs in
the yard, your friends at their cabins at the lake. Little
did you know that 2,500 years ago, in a Grecian meadow
redolent with oregano, a child like you spun his yo-yo
while sheep grazed around him. A Filipino boy hunting
with his father threw a studded, sharp-edged yo-yo at a
wild pig.

Yours was one of the 45 million flying out of stores in
towns and cities across the continent in the sixties. You
adapted it to your height by adjusting the string; the offi-
cial length was the distance between the ground and your
belly button. All day long, you taught yourself the tricks:

Around the World, Walk the Dog, Sleep. The yo-yo fit into your palm, or you could carry it in your pocket beside your jackknife. Yo-yo-ing was something you could do without a captain or a team; it was a movement as close to stasis as it could get. You could daydream and yo-yo, you could walk a real dog and yo-yo, you could spin it while you were eating with your family, hand under the table. Once during dinner you whacked your father's shin, and he threatened to smash the yo-yo with a hammer. You mowed the grass for two weeks to get it back.

Your grade five teacher collected all the yo-yos every morning and returned them after school. One day the boy you yo-yoed with by the monkey bars became more important than the toy itself. Your body yearned to learn new tricks, you needed both your hands, the yo-yo languished. Years later, you learned it was the first toy to make it into outer space. Those who planned the mission in Cape Canaveral must have known its name comes from the Tagalog spoken in the Philippines and means, heart-breakingly, "come back."

ZIPPER

1. Many are skittish around zippers. In their childhood, a nub of flesh was snagged and torn. Or perhaps their agitation comes from the zipper's tyranny of symmetry, its single-mindedness. Cold as scissors, obdurate in its habits, overly binary and precise. With more teeth than a tiger, its parallel jaws lock together. You can see why the sound of a zipper, especially in a room at night, evokes the jitters. All across the world, in every city, there are tailors who make a living from converting metal or plastic tracks to hooks and eyes, to loops, to buttons, to Velcro strips.

2. Though dependent on you to bring their two halves together, zippers are never obsequious. If they're meant to close a sweater, their power of persuasion lies with the cold. If they function as a fly, they use your fear of embarrassment and shame. Zippers are known for their aloofness, their indifference, though in many garments they lie next to the heart. In their common place on trousers they're overly familiar with the genitals, especially the pulling out and the tucking in, but in their own coupling, they remain mechanical, strangely unaroused.

3. They're sexiest on the back of a dress a woman can't do up on her own. She lifts the hair on her neck and arches her back while someone behind her slowly pulls the metal tag up over vertebra after vertebra to the top. Often, the next step is to pull the tag down. Zippers are most ugly on a pair of rubber overshoes, most pragmatic on the canvas door of a tent. To them, openness means incompleteness. Like Poirot and Holmes, they link the pieces, they sum up, the last clue falling into place with a perfect, tiny click.

4. Void of human feeling, of the need to gossip. You can depend on them to keep a secret. They've been hiding what lies beneath the cloth for close to a hundred years. Though the zipper was invented, as we know it, in 1914, in Meadville, Pennsylvania, Canada has claimed the zipper as its own. The man who secured the U.S. patent ran a company in Ontario that churned out more zippers than did our southern neighbour or Japan. In 2007 the zipper was voted eighth on CBC's list of the Greatest Canadian Inventions. When you think of all a zipper holds together—what a metaphor for our nation—it's shocking it ranked lower than five-pin bowling and the Wonderbra.

5. Around 200 BC, the zipper entered human thought. Euclid of Alexandria was writing *The Elements.* Scholars swear his masterpiece in thirteen volumes is about abstract mathematics, but you can see, just below Euclid's consciousness, the form of the zipper taking shape. Look at two of his twenty-three definitions: 2. a line is breadth-less length, and 4. a straight line is a line which lies evenly with the points on itself. Had he been a more practical man, the zipper wouldn't have had to wait almost two thousand years to turn into matter. It could have been a central element of the toga. It could have been drawn between two points on a winter robe made of sheepskin. Note the last of Euclid's five common notions: The whole is greater than the part. Is there anything that demonstrates the concept more elegantly than a zipper, zipping shut?

NOTES

ALLUSIONS, SUBTLE NODS and the sources of
unidentified quotations:

William Wordsworth ("Book"); William Shakespeare,
Dannie Abse ("Brain"); Gertrude Stein, Raymond
Chandler ("Button"); Russell Edson ("Ceiling"); James
Orchard Halliwell-Phillipps ("Chin"); Mordecai Richler
("Starts with the Letter *K*"); William Shakespeare
("Dictionary"); Bob Dylan ("Eraser"); Melanie Siebert
("Feet"); Robert Frost ("Fork"); Oliver Sacks, René
Magritte, Lewis Carroll, Patrick Lane (AKA Rex Titter)
("Hat"); William Shakespeare ("Hinge"); Gabriel García
Márquez ("Ice"); Italo Calvino, William Shakespeare,
Guy Vanderhaeghe, the Book of Genesis ("Lamp");
Robert Frost ("Measure"); William Carlos Williams,
Wallace Stevens ("Objects"); Robert Frost ("Shoe");
Peggy Shumaker ("Vagina"); William Carlos Williams
("Wheelbarrow").

ACKNOWLEDGEMENTS

EPIGRAPHS: The Francis Ponge quotation originated in *View,* series 4, no. 4, November 1945. The version I've used was translated by Robert Bly; I apologize for my failure to keep track of where Bly's version first appeared. Edouard Levé's description of the dictionary is from "Life in Three Houses" in *Suicide,* Dalkey Archive Press, 2011. It was translated from the French by Jan Steyn and published in *Harper's Magazine,* April 2011. The source of the Yogi Berra quote was rinkworks.com/said/yogiberra.shtml.

"Button," "Clothes Hanger" and "Chair" appeared in *cv2;* "Ironing Board" in *The Associative Press;* "Bowl," "Shakers" and "Kitchen Sink" in *Cuizine;* "Coffee Pot," "Bicycle" and "Doorknob" in *PRISM international.* "Doorknob" received the Earle Birney Poetry Prize, the editor's choice for the best poem published in *PRISM international* in 2010. "Brain" appeared in the anthology *In the Flesh,* published by Brindle & Glass in the spring of 2012.

This book owes much to the sharp editorial eye of Barbara Pulling, a genius at cutting, correcting my stumbles and mistakes and nudging me to go further than I thought I could go. I want to thank Rob Sanders of Greystone Books for his faith in me. My writing life and my life in general are immeasurably enriched by the love and support of my husband, Patrick Lane. The University of Victoria assisted me with research funding, and the Saskatchewan Writers' Guild Writers/Artists Retreat offered me the quietude necessary to draft the pieces that make up this book. There, over many years, I've benefited from the friendship and encouragement of my fellow writers Anne Carter, Sandra Campbell, Liz Philips, Annette LeBox and Jane Munro, and that of Father Demetrius and Abbot Peter. Finally, I'd like to thank the many readers who have been in touch with me about my books over the years. You make everything worthwhile.